LA LUMIÈRE DU SOLEIL

(The Light of the Sun)

Amy Fazni

Balboa Press books may be ordered through booksellers or by contacting:

Balboa Press
A Division of Hay House
1663 Liberty Drive
Bloomington, IN 47403
www.balboapress.com
1 (877) 407-4847

ISBN: 978-1-9822-2001-3 (sc)
ISBN: 978-1-9822-2002-0 (e)

Library of Congress Control Number: 2019903483

Print information available on the last page.

Balboa Press rev. date: 04/12/2019

BALBOA
PRESS
A DIVISION OF HAY HOUSE

For my beautiful children, Rhett, Hunter, and Elle. I love you as the sun loves the earth.

I am afraid of the dark.

So I asked the darkness, "darkness will you please go away? I am afraid of you."

The darkness did not go away.

So I asked the darkness nicely, "darkness, please go away. I am afraid of you."

The darkness still would not go away.

So I begged the darkness, "darkness, will you please, *please* go away? I am so afraid of you!"

The darkness would not go away,
so I cried and cried and cried
until I cried myself to sleep.

I awoke to a beautiful ray of sunshine
shining through my window.

"Momma, momma, last night I asked the darkness to go away. I asked it nicely, I even begged the darkness to please go away. The darkness wouldn't go away, so I cried and cried and cried until I cried myself to sleep!"

My momma said, "my dear Sunshine, the darkness will not go away when you ask it to, ask it nicely, or even beg it to go away."

when you bring l
MAGI
disappears

ht, the darkness

ALLY

ll by itself

Printed in the United States
By Bookmasters